# Walking in Love: Wedding Vows for that Special Day

*(Caminando en el amor: votos de boda para ese día especial)*

Terri L. McCrea, M.Ed., LPC

Walking in Love:
Wedding Vows for that Special Day
(Caminando en el amor: Votos matrimoniales para ese día especial)

Cassaundra Mulligan, Editor (Editora)
Translation by Magaly Torres (Traducción por Magaly Torres)
Cover quote of Nikki Giovanni referencing *The Heart of a Man and Poems by Terri (On Love, Life and Destinies)*

ISBN-13: 978-0-9801052-6-1
ISBN-10: 0-9801052-6-9

Cover and interior arrangements by Kathrine Rend – Rend Graphics
Portada y arreglos interiores por Kathrine Rend - Rend Graphics
www.rendgraphics.com

Printed in the United States of America.
Impreso en los Estados Unidos de América.

How to Contact the Author:
Poetic Expressions by Terri
Terri L. McCrea, M.Ed., LPC, LPC/S
1643 B Savannah Highway, #113 Charleston, SC 29407
Mobile (843) 437-7572/Fax (843) 763-7202
poeticexpressions@att.net

Attention colleges, universities, corporations, organizations, persons and writing and publishing organizations: Quantity discounts are available on bulk purchases of this manuscript for educational training purposes, fund-raising, or gift giving. Special poems, gift sets, books, or book excerpts can also be created to fit your specific needs.

Atención a colegios, universidades, corporaciones, organizaciones, personas y organizaciones de redacción y editoriales: hay descuentos por cantidad disponibles en compras a granel de este manuscrito con fines de capacitación educativa, recaudación de fondos o regalos. También se pueden crear poemas especiales, juegos de regalos, libros o extractos de libros para satisfacer sus necesidades específicas.

# Walking in Love: Wedding Vows for that Special Day

(Caminando en el amor:
votos de boda para ese día especial)

# Introduction

The poems in *Walking in Love: Wedding Vows for that Special Day* were created because frantic couples stated that after choosing the date, the venue, the wedding colors, the cake, the attire, the wedding program, the officiant, the bridesmaids, the groomsmen, the honeymoon location and the food they realized they forgot one thing, their marriage vows.

I love that 21$^{st}$ Century couples are opting to write personal vows versus repeating traditional marriage vows. I think personal vows are intimate, touching and sentimental.

So here's a few you can choose from to make your wedding a special day. I sincerely hope my love poems capture what you want to say but just don't know how.

I would like to thank Magaly Torres, Billie James, Kasia Ciszewski, Elmo, Cassaundra Mulligan and all those who supported and inspired *Walking in Love: Wedding Vows for that Special Day.*

# Introducción

Los poemas en *Caminando en el amor: los votos matrimoniales para ese día especial* fueron creados porque las parejas frenéticas declararon que después de elegir la fecha, el lugar, los colores de la boda, el pastel, el atuendo, el programa de la boda, el oficiante, las damas de honor, los padrinos de boda, la ubicación de la luna de miel y la comida que se dieron cuenta de que olvidaron una cosa, sus votos matrimoniales.

Me encanta que parejas del siglo 21 están optando por escribir votos personales en vez de repetir votos matrimoniales tradicionales. Creo que los votos personales son íntimos, emotivos y sentimentales.

Así que aquí hay algunos de los que puedes elegir para hacer de tu boda un día especial. Espero sinceramente que mis poemas de amor capten lo que quieres decir, pero no sabes cómo.

Me gustaría agradecer a Magaly Torres, Billie James, Kasia Ciszewski, Elmo, Cassaundra Mulligan y a todos los que apoyaron e inspiraron *Caminando en el amor: los votos matrimoniales para ese día especial.*

# Contents (Contenido)

# Us

## Nosotros )

(You can choose to omit the poems title as you read your vow or use the inspiration page to write your own.)

~~~~~

(Puedes elegir omitir el título de los poemas mientras lees tu voto o usar la página de inspiración para escribir tu propio.)

# You and I

I love it when we laugh.
I love it when we dance.

I've loved being your woman.
I've loved being your man.

I love our true love.
I love our lovey-dovey romance.

I love that we took that leap of faith.
I love that we took that once in a lifetime chance.

I love your tenderness.
I love your lovestruck eyes.

I love our love story.
I love our you and I.

# Tú y yo

Me encanta cuando nos reímos.
Me encanta cuando bailamos.

Me encanta ser tu mujer.
Me encanta ser tu hombre.

Amo a nuestro verdadero amor.
Me encanta nuestro amoroso romance.

Me encanta que hayamos dado ese salto de fe.
Me encanta que aprovechamos esa oportunidad única en la vida.

Amo tu ternura.
Me encantan tus ojos enamorados.

Me encanta nuestra historia de amor.
Me encanta nuestro tú y yo.

# You and I

Share what you personally love about one another:

_____
_____
_____
_____
_____
_____
_____
_____
_____
_____
_____
_____
_____
_____
_____
_____
_____
_____
_____
_____

# Tú y yo

Compartan lo que aman personalmente el uno del otro:

_____

_____

_____

_____

_____

_____

_____

_____

_____

_____

_____

_____

_____

_____

_____

_____

_____

_____

_____

_____

_____

_____

_____

# I'm Forever Grateful II

I'm forever grateful
for all of life's tests,
for it made me the vessel
that stands before you,
giving life its absolute best.

I now walk in purpose,
love,
truth
and faith,
settling for nothing less,
as I choose you as my soulmate.

# Estoy por siempre agradecido II

Estoy por siempre agradecido(a)
por todas las pruebas de la vida,
porque me convirtió en el recipiente
que está ante ti,
dando lo mejor a la vida.

Ahora camino en el propósito,
el amor,
la verdad
y la fe, y no me
conformo con nada menos,
ya que te elijo como mi alma gemela.

# I'm Forever Grateful II

Share what you are grateful for in each other:

_____
_____
_____
_____
_____
_____
_____
_____
_____
_____
_____
_____
_____
_____
_____
_____
_____
_____
_____
_____
_____
_____
_____

# Estoy por siempre agradecido(a) II

Compartan por lo que estan agradecidos de cada uno:

# True Love

True Love Flows to the Heart.
True Love Vacillates through the Mind.
True Love is Vulnerable.
True Love is Kind.

True Love is a Look.
True Love is Give and Take.
True Love is Sweet Words.
True Love is Touching Tender Moments
Each and Every Day.

True Love is Forever.
True Love is Pink, Violet and Red Hues.
True Love is a Gift.
True Love is You.

# El amor Verdadero

El amor verdadero fluye hacia el corazón.
El amor verdadero vacila a través de la mente.
El amor verdadero es vulnerable.
El amor verdadero es amable.

El amor verdadero es una mirada.
El amor verdadero es dar y tomar.
El amor verdadero son palabras dulces.
El amor verdadero es tocar los momentos tiernos
todos los días.

El amor verdadero es para siempre.
El amor verdadero es de tonos rosado, violeta y rojo.
El amor verdadero es un regalo.
El amor verdadero eres tú.

# True Love

What does true love mean to you?

_____
_____
_____
_____
_____
_____
_____
_____
_____
_____
_____
_____
_____
_____
_____
_____
_____
_____
_____
_____
_____

# El amor verdadero

¿Qué significa para ti el verdadero amor?

_____

_____

_____

_____

_____

_____

_____

_____

_____

_____

_____

_____

_____

_____

_____

_____

_____

_____

_____

_____

_____

_____

# Definition of a Friend

You've been there through the darkness.
You've been there through the storms.
You've been there through the trials.
You've been there through it all.

You've walked my miles.
You've dried my tears.

This Definition of a Friend is You.

# Definición de un(a) amigo(a)

Has estado allí a través de la oscuridad.
Has estado allí a través de las tormentas.
Has estado allí a través de las pruebas.
Has estado allí a través de todo esto.

Has caminado mis millas.
Has secado mis lágrimas.

Esta definición de un(a) amigo(a) eres tú.

# Definition of a Friend

What meaningful qualities make
your soulmate a true friend?

_____
_____
_____
_____
_____
_____
_____
_____
_____
_____
_____
_____
_____
_____
_____
_____
_____
_____
_____

# Definición de un(a) amigo(a)

¿Qué cualidades significativas hacen de
tu alma gemela un verdadero amigo?

# The One

I can't thank the Universe enough,
for uniting what was worlds apart.

I can't thank the Universe enough,
for entrusting me with such a pure and caring heart.

I can't thank the Universe enough,
for hearing my prayers and cries.

I can't thank the Universe enough,
for my powder blue sky.

I can't thank the Universe enough,
for bequeathing me with true love.

I can't thank the Universe enough,
for blessing me with my very own kissing dove.

I can't thank the Universe enough,
for allowing me to see the stars,
the moon and the sun.

I can't thank the Universe enough,
for blessing me with *the one*.

# El Único

No puedo agradecer lo suficiente al Universo,
por unir lo que era mundos aparte.

No puedo agradecer lo suficiente al Universo,
por confiarme un corazón tan puro y cariñoso.

No puedo agradecer lo suficiente al Universo,
por escuchar mis oraciones y llantos.

No puedo agradecer lo suficiente al Universo,
por mi cielo azul claro.

No puedo agradecer lo suficiente al Universo
por haberme legado con amor verdadero.

No puedo agradecer lo suficiente al Universo,
por bendecirme con mi propia paloma besándose.

No puedo agradecer lo suficiente al Universo,
por permitirme ver las estrellas,
la luna y el sol.

No puedo agradecer lo suficiente al Universo,
por bendecirme con *el único/ la única*.

# The One

What makes your true love special and unique?

_____

_____

_____

_____

_____

_____

_____

_____

_____

_____

_____

_____

_____

_____

_____

_____

_____

_____

_____

_____

# El Único

¿Qué hace que tu amor verdadero sea especial y único?

_____

_____

_____

_____

_____

_____

_____

_____

_____

_____

_____

_____

_____

_____

_____

_____

_____

_____

_____

_____

*Love*

You are my king.
You are my queen.

You are my knight in shining armour.
You are my dream.

I promise to cherish our *us*.
I promise to be your friend.

I promise to treasure our *we*.
I promise the same until the very end.

# Amor

Tu eres mi rey.
Tu eres mi reina.

Eres mi caballero de brillante armadura.
Eres mi sueño.

Prometo apreciar a nuestros *nosotros*.
Prometo ser tu amigo(a).

Prometo atesorar nuestro *nosotros*.
Prometo lo mismo hasta el final.

*Love*

Share love promises from the heart:

# Amor

Comparte promesas de amor del corazón:

_____

_____

_____

_____

_____

_____

_____

_____

_____

_____

_____

_____

_____

_____

_____

_____

_____

_____

_____

_____

# Déjà Vu

I fell in love with your mind.
I fell in love with your beautiful smile.

I fell in love with your tender words.
I fell in love with an ethereal songbird.

I fell in love with you.
I fell in love with my déjà vu.

# Déjà Vu

Me enamoré de tu mente.
Me enamoré de tu hermosa sonrisa.

Me enamoré de tus tiernas palabras.
Me enamoré de un pájaro cantor etéreo.

Me enamoré de ti.
Me enamoré de mi déjà vu.

# Déjà Vu

Share glimpses of your love story:

_____
_____
_____
_____
_____
_____
_____
_____
_____
_____
_____
_____
_____
_____
_____
_____
_____
_____
_____
_____
_____
_____
_____

# Déjà Vu

Comparte destellos de tu historia de amor:

_____
_____
_____
_____
_____
_____
_____
_____
_____
_____
_____
_____
_____
_____
_____
_____
_____
_____
_____
_____
_____
_____

# Destined Love

Strolling
atop soothing sands,
under smiling crescent moons,
is when I knew
that our union
was destined love.

# Amor Destinado

Paseando por
arenas tranquilas,
bajo lunas crecientes sonrientes,
es cuando supe
que nuestra unión
era amor destinado.

# Destined Love

Share memories of the first time you met:

_____

_____

_____

_____

_____

_____

_____

_____

_____

_____

_____

_____

_____

_____

_____

_____

_____

_____

_____

_____

_____

# Amor Destinado

Comparte recuerdos de la primera vez que se conocieron:

_____
_____
_____
_____
_____
_____
_____
_____
_____
_____
_____
_____
_____
_____
_____
_____
_____
_____
_____
_____
_____

# *Marriage*

I vow to always support you,
and satisfy throughout.

I vow to always be present,
day in and day out.

I vow to always shelter you,
when the bottom falls out.

I vow to not only respect, but more importantly,
understand you, inside and out.

I vow to always connect with you,
to eliminate any doubts.

I vow to always compromise,
treasure our union and walk as one.

Because I undeniably know,
that you are my true love.

# Matrimonio

Prometo siempre apoyarte,
y satisfacerte en todo momento.

Prometo estar siempre presente,
día tras día.

Prometo protegerte siempre,
cuando el fondo se caiga.

Prometo no solo respetar, sino lo que es más importante,
entenderte, por dentro y por fuera.

Prometo conectarme siempre contigo,
para eliminar cualquier duda.

Prometo siempre transigir,
atesorar nuestra unión y caminar como uno solo.

Porque sin duda sé,
que eres mi verdadero amor.

# *Marriage*

Share what marriage means to you:

_____
_____
_____
_____
_____
_____
_____
_____
_____
_____
_____
_____
_____
_____
_____
_____
_____
_____
_____
_____

# Matrimonio

Comparte lo que significa el matrimonio para ti:

_____

_____

_____

_____

_____

_____

_____

_____

_____

_____

_____

_____

_____

_____

_____

_____

_____

_____

_____

_____

_____

# Love Me

Love me,

not less than,

not more than,

but

as much as

I love you.

# Amame

Amame,

no menos que,

no más que,

pero

tanto como

yo te amo.

# Love Me

What are your most important marriage
needs, wants and desires?

# *Amame*

Cuales son tus matrimonios mas importantes
necesidades, deseos y deseos?

_____
_____
_____
_____
_____
_____
_____
_____
_____
_____
_____
_____
_____
_____
_____
_____
_____
_____
_____
_____
_____
_____
_____

# I've Found

# The One

I've found *the one*
who's in tune with
my desires, my humor and my esteem.

I've found *the one*
who's in tune with
my life calling, my purpose and my dreams.

I've found *the one*
who's in tune with
my past, my pain and my tears.

I've found *the one*
who's in tune with
my thoughts, my feelings and my fears.

I've found *the one*
who's in tune with
my touch, my journey and my sensitivity.

I've found *the one*
who's in tune with
my heartbeat, my soul and my spirituality.

I've found *the one* who I get and who gets me.

# He encontrado el único/ la única para mi

He encontrado *el único/ la única*
que está en sintonía con
mis deseos, mi humor y mi estima.

He encontrado *el único/ la única*
que está en sintonía con
mi vocación de vida, mi propósito y mis sueños.

He encontrado *el único/ la única*
que está en sintonía con
mi pasado, mi dolor y mis lágrimas.

He encontrado *el único/ la única*
que está en sintonía con
mis pensamientos, mis sentimientos y mis miedos.

He encontrado *el único/ la única*
que está en sintonía con
mi toque, mi viaje y mi sensibilidad.

He encontrado *el único/ la única*
que está en sintonía con
el latido de mi corazón, mi alma y mi espiritualidad.

He encontrado *el único/ la única* a quién entiendo y me entiende a mi.

# I've Found
# The One

Share moments of when you knew
your true love was the one:

_____
_____
_____
_____
_____
_____
_____
_____
_____
_____
_____
_____
_____
_____
_____
_____
_____
_____
_____
_____
_____

# He encontrado
## el único/ la única para mi

Comparte momentos de cuando supiste que tu amor verdadero
era el único/ la única para ti:

_____

_____

_____

_____

_____

_____

_____

_____

_____

_____

_____

_____

_____

_____

_____

_____

_____

_____

_____

*Love is...*

Love is Withstanding,
Patient,
Authentic
and Free.

Love is Priceless,
Forever and Genuine,
for Love is the Key.

Love is Effortless,
Heartwarming,
Special,
and True.

Love is Forgiving,
Selfless,
Tender...

Love is You.

# El amor es...

El Amor es Resistente,
Paciente,
Auténtico
y Gratuito.

El Amor No Tiene Precio,
es Por Siempre y Genuino,
porque el Amor es la Clave.

El Amor es Sin Esfuerzo,
es Reconfortante,
Especial
y Verdadero.

El Amor Perdona,
es Desinteresado,
Tierno...

El Amor eres Tú.

# Love is...

## What does love mean to you?

# El amor es...

¿Qué significa el amor para tí?

_____

_____

_____

_____

_____

_____

_____

_____

_____

_____

_____

_____

_____

_____

_____

_____

_____

_____

_____

_____

_____

_____

# We Know Love

We know love because...

We've received it in our minds;

We've nurtured it in our souls;

It's touched our hearts;

We've walked with it in the rain;

We've respected it's power;

We've chosen it as our guide;

We've treasured it through the miles;

We've seen it in smitten eyes;

We've embraced it like our cherished life and

it's made us feel like the luckiest person alive.

# Conocemos el amor

Conocemos el amor porque...

Lo hemos recibido en nuestras mentes;

Lo hemos nutrido en nuestras almas;

Ha tocado nuestros corazones;

Hemos caminado con él bajo la lluvia;

Hemos respetado su poder;

Lo hemos elegido como nuestro guía;

Lo hemos atesorado a través de las millas;

Lo hemos visto en los ojos enamorados;

Lo hemos adoptado como nuestra preciada vida y

nos ha hecho sentir como la persona más afortunada del mundo.

# We Know Love

Share how love has touched and changed your life:

# Conocemos el amor

Comparte cómo el amor ha tocado y cambiado tu vida:

_____

_____

_____

_____

_____

_____

_____

_____

_____

_____

_____

_____

_____

_____

_____

_____

_____

_____

_____

_____

_____

# I Love You

From the first day we met,
there hasn't been one day,
not one day of regret.

You inspire, empower and
bring out my absolute best.

Since that first day we met,
I've had a permanent smile.

I love when you are the recipient
of my accidental pocket dials.

There was never a day
I didn't see our future in your eyes.

I've been on top of the world
since the day you said
yes, yes, yes
to being my wife.

# Te amo

Desde el primer día que nos conocimos,
no ha habido un día,
ni un solo día de arrepentimiento.

Tú inspiras, empoderas y
sacas lo mejor de mí.

Desde el primer día que nos conocimos,
he tenido una sonrisa permanente.

Me encanta cuando eres el destinatario
de mis llamadas accidentales.

Nunca hubo un día
que no viera nuestro futuro en tus ojos.

He estado en la cima del mundo
desde el día que dijiste
sí, sí, sí
a ser mi esposa.

# I Love You

Share the moment you first heard *I Love You*:

_____

# Te amo

Comparte el momento que escuchaste por primera vez *te amo*:

# Her

## (Ella)

(The poems in this section are to be read by the woman. You can choose to read the entire poem or use the inspiration page to write your own.)

(Los poemas de esta sección deben ser leídos por la mujer. Puedes elegir leer todo el poema o usar la página de inspiración para escribir la tuya.)

# Not in a Million Years

Who would've thought
one Indian summer –
this delicate petal
would find a heavenly love.

Who would've thought a selfish prayer
would bless this bright eyed dreamer
with such a sweet love.

Who would've thought
a wish upon a star
would bless this hopeless romantic
with an unconditional,
pure and organic love,
that she can forever and always trust.

Not in a Million Years

# Ni en un millón de años

Quién hubiera pensado que
un verano indio -
este delicado pétalo
encontraría un amor celestial.

¿Quién hubiera pensado que una oración egoísta
bendeciría a este soñador de ojos brillantes
con un amor tan dulce?

¿Quién hubiera pensado que
un deseo sobre una estrella
bendeciría a esta romántica desesperada
con un incondicional,
puro y orgánico amor,
en cual ella puede siempre y para siempre confiar.

No en un millón de años

# Not in a Million Years

Share how you know your true love was heaven sent:

# Ni en un millón de años

Comparte cómo sabes que tu amor verdadero fue enviado del cielo:

_____

_____

_____

_____

_____

_____

_____

_____

_____

_____

_____

_____

_____

_____

_____

_____

_____

_____

_____

_____

_____

# The Joy of a Man

I care about your passions
and about your days.
I value your thoughts and
what you have to say.

There's never a day
you don't surprise.
There's never a day
you don't make
this smitten school girl
all giddy inside.

I knew you were the one
from your actions, words and deeds.
I knew you were the one
by how you loved me
just as I am.

# La alegría de un hombre

Me importan tus pasiones
y tus días.
Valoro tus pensamientos y
lo que tienes que decir.

Nunca hay un día
que no me sorprendas.
Nunca hay un día en el
que no dejes a
esta colegiala
mareada por dentro.

Sabía que eras el indicado
por tus acciones, palabras y hechos.
Sabía que eras quien
me amaba
tal como soy.

# The Joy of a Man

Share how your true love makes you smile:

_____

_____

_____

_____

_____

_____

_____

_____

_____

_____

_____

_____

_____

_____

_____

_____

_____

_____

_____

_____

_____

_____

# La alegría de un hombre

Comparte cómo tu amor verdadero te hace sonreír:

# I Never Knew

I never knew a love could matter.
I never knew a love could care.
I never knew a love could capture.
I never knew a love so dear.
I never knew a love could withstand.
I never knew, until you asked for my hand.

# Nunca supe

Nunca supe que un amor podría importar.
Nunca supe que un amor pudiera preocupar.
Nunca supe que un amor pudiera capturar.
Nunca conocí un amor tan querido.
Nunca supe que un amor pudiera soportar.
Nunca lo supe, hasta que pediste mi mano.

# I Never Knew

Share memories of the marriage proposal:

_____

_____

_____

_____

_____

_____

_____

_____

_____

_____

_____

_____

_____

_____

_____

_____

_____

_____

_____

_____

# Nunca supe

Comparte recuerdos de la propuesta de matrimonio:

# Him

## (Él)

(The poems in this section are to be read by the man. You can choose to read the entire poem or use the inspiration page to write your own.)

⌒

(Los poemas de esta sección deben ser leídos por el hombre. Puedes elegir leer todo el poema o usar la página de inspiración para escribir la tuya.)

# Black Butterfly

From out of nowhere,
not a canary yellow,
a turquoise blue or
fiery mango
but a beautiful black butterfly.

A wondrous vision.
A sign of hope.
An anomaly.
A symbol of joy.

So blessed to be graced
with a miracle,
that's touched this kindled heart and
is forever embedded in this kindled mind.

# Mariposa negra

De la nada,
no un amarillo canario,
un azul turquesa o un
mango ardiente
sino una hermosa mariposa negra.

Una maravillosa visión.
Una señal de esperanza.
Una anomalía.
Un símbolo de alegría.

Tan bendecido de ser agraciado
con un milagro,
que ha tocado este corazón encendido y
está siempre incrustado en esta mente encendida.

# Black Butterfly

Compare your loved one with something beautiful in nature - and why?

_____
_____
_____
_____
_____
_____
_____
_____
_____
_____
_____
_____
_____
_____
_____
_____
_____
_____
_____
_____
_____

# Mariposa negra

Compara a tu ser querido con algo hermoso en la naturaleza,
¿y por qué?

# Soul Mate

In traveling the world,
to my wonderment found,
my sun, my moon,
let me continue to expound.

An irresistible creature,
who was right under my nose.
You're my Mondial, my Morisque,
you're my Nightingale rose.

You're much more than a friend.
You're a blessing in disguise.
You're my porcelain doll.
You're my beautiful butterfly.

You're my princess, my queen.
You're my sweet dream.

You're my right hand and more than enough,
for this one woman man.

You're my sanctuary, my summer love.
You're my eternity, my forever,
You're a gift from above.

# Alma gemela

Al viajar por el mundo,
para mi asombro he encontrado,
mi sol, mi luna,
permítanme continuar exponiendo.

Una criatura irresistible,
que estaba justo debajo de mi nariz.
Eres mi Mondial, mi Morisque,
eres mi ruiseñor rosa.

Eres mucho más que una amiga.
Eres una bendición disfrazada.
Eres mi muñeca de porcelana.
Eres mi hermosa mariposa.

Eres mi princesa, mi reina.
Eres mi dulce sueño.

Eres mi mano derecha y más que suficiente,
para este hombre de una mujer.

Eres mi santuario, mi amor de verano.
Eres mi eternidad, mi para siempre,
Eres un regalo de arriba.

# Soul Mate

Share moments of when you knew
your true love was your forever:

_____
_____
_____
_____
_____
_____
_____
_____
_____
_____
_____
_____
_____
_____
_____
_____
_____
_____
_____

# Alma gemela

Comparte momentos de cuando supiste
que tu amor verdadero era tu por siempre:

_____
_____
_____
_____
_____
_____
_____
_____
_____
_____
_____
_____
_____
_____
_____
_____
_____
_____
_____
_____
_____
_____

# Wedding Day

The search for my soul mate is over,
for I've finally found my wife.

I knew the moment you walked down the aisle,
that I would break down and cry.

My queen, I'm overcome with pride,
as you have graciously
chosen me to be your king.

My queen, it would be an honour
that you not only take my last name
but more importantly,
accept this ring,
as a symbol of our love,
on our wedding day.

# Día de la boda

La búsqueda de mi alma gemela ha terminado,
porque finalmente encontré a mi esposa.

Sabía que en el momento en que caminabas por el pasillo,
me derrumbaría y lloraría.

Mi reina, estoy lleno de orgullo,
ya que me has amablemente
elegido para ser tu rey.

Mi reina, sería un honor
que no solo tomes mi apellido,
sino lo que es más importante,
aceptar este anillo,
símbolo de nuestro amor,
el día de nuestra boda.

# Wedding Day

Share touching moments from the planning of the wedding up to the wedding day:

_____

_____

_____

_____

_____

_____

_____

_____

_____

_____

_____

_____

_____

_____

_____

_____

_____

_____

_____

# Día de la boda

Comparte momentos conmovedores desde la planificación de la boda hasta el día de la boda:

_____
_____
_____
_____
_____
_____
_____
_____
_____
_____
_____
_____
_____
_____
_____
_____
_____
_____
_____
_____
_____
_____

# I Love How You

I love how you encourage me
when I'm down on my luck.
I love how you believe in me
with unwavering trust.

I love how you warm my soul
with your dreamy eyes.
I love how you praise me
when I wholeheartedly try.

I love how you are my rainbow
after the storm.
I love how you comfort
in times of sorrow, grief and mourn.

I love how you are always a shoulder
in which this weary head can lean.
I love how you are always present
as we live out our wildest dreams.

I love how you love me unconditionally.
I love how you maintain your faith in me.

I love how you encourage
when I fail or fall.
I love how you are my cheerleader
when I give it my all.

I love how you stick by me
through the best and worst of times.
I love knowing I am blessed with my forever,
my always, my endearing Valentine.

# Me encanta cómo a ti

Me encanta cómo me animas
cuando tengo mala suerte.
Me encanta cómo crees en mí
con una confianza inquebrantable.

Me encanta cómo calientas mi alma
con tus dreme ojos.
Me encanta cómo me alabas
cuando lo intento de todo corazón.

Me encanta como eres mi arcoiris
después de la tormenta.
Me encanta cómo me consuelas
en momentos de pena, pena y luto.

Me encanta cómo eres siempre un hombro
en el que esta cabeza cansada puede inclinarse.
Me encanta cómo siempre estás presente
mientras vivimos nuestros sueños más salvajes.

Me encanta como me amas incondicionalmente.
Me encanta cómo mantienes tu fe en mí.

Me encanta cómo me animas
cuando fallo o caigo.
Me encanta cómo eres mi animadora
cuando doy mi todo.

Me encanta cómo te quedas conmigo
en los mejores y peores momentos.
Me encanta saber soy bendecido con mi por siempre,
mi entrañable, San Valentín.

# I Love How You

Share that moment when you fell in love:

_____
_____
_____
_____
_____
_____
_____
_____
_____
_____
_____
_____
_____
_____
_____
_____
_____
_____
_____

# Me encanta cómo a ti

Comparte ese momento cuando te enamoraste:

# Sweet Dream

I prayed for the day,
our eyes would lock,
as they did in my sweet dream.

I prepared a home,
as my faith continued on,
while patiently waiting for thee.

As I trusted, prayed and believed,
you appeared,
stealing my breath and buckling my knees.

Not until you said yes,
to be my wife,
did I believe you were real,

like the majestic images of post card mountain peaks,
like God's awesome presence in mystical canyon cores
and like the healing powers of topaz marvelled seas.

A day never passes,
that I don't thank the Universe
for making my sweet dream a reality.

# Dulce sueño

Recé por el día,
que nuestros ojos se conectarían,
como lo hicieron en mi dulce sueño.

Preparé un hogar,
mientras mi fe continuaba,
mientras esperaba pacientemente por ti.

Mientras confiaba, oraba y creía,
apareciste,
robándome el aliento y doblando las rodillas.

Hasta que no dijeras que sí,
a ser mi esposa,
creí que eras real,

como las majestuosas imágenes de los picos de las montañas,
como la asombrosa presencia de Dios en los núcleos del cañón
místico
y al igual que los poderes curativos de los mares topacios
maravillados.

Un día nunca pasa,
que no agradezco al Universo
por hacer realidad mi dulce sueño.

# Sweet Dream

Share your marriage vision:

_____
_____
_____
_____
_____
_____
_____
_____
_____
_____
_____
_____
_____
_____
_____
_____
_____
_____
_____
_____
_____

# Dulce sueño

Comparte tu visión de matrimonio:

_____
_____
_____
_____
_____
_____
_____
_____
_____
_____
_____
_____
_____
_____
_____
_____
_____
_____
_____
_____

# The Joy of a Woman

Love at first sight.

I only knew it to be true,
and not a myth,
on the day you came into my life.

I knew you were heaven sent,
because you looked not at me,
but deep into my soul.

I knew you were heaven sent,
from your incandescent glow.

I love how you love me, just as I am.
It feels like home when I hold your hand.

Despite distance and time,
all that will ever matter is you.

# La alegría de una mujer

Amor a primera vista.

Solo supe que era verdad,
y no un mito,
en el día que entraste en mi vida.

Sabía que fuiste enviada del cielo,
porque no me viste a mi,
sino a lo profundo de mi alma.

Sabia que fuiste enviada del cielo,
de tu incandescente brillo.

Me encanta como me amas, tal como soy.
Se siente como un hogar cuando sostengo tu mano.

A pesar de la distancia y el tiempo,
todo lo que siempre importa eres tú.

# The Joy of a Woman

Share what makes your true love one of a kind:

# La alegría de una mujer

Comparte lo que hace que tu amor verdadero
sea único en su clase:

# Nightingale Rose

I embarked on a voyage,
throwing caution to the wind,
to hold one of earth's rarest bloom.

Despite monstrous storms, frigid nights
and thrashing monsoons,
I found my peace—
my wife,
my dream,
my joy,
a friend
and my Nightingale Rose.

# Rosa Ruiseñor

Me embarqué en un viaje,
lanzando precaución al viento,
para aguantar una de las floraciones más raras de la tierra.

A pesar de las tormentas monstruosas,
las noches frías
y los monzones,
encontré mi paz
mi esposa,
mi sueño,
mi alegría,
una amiga
y mi rosa ruiseñor.

# Nightingale Rose

Like a flower, your love will bloom. Share your hopes and
dreams for the future of your marriage garden!

# Rosa Ruiseñor

Como una flor, tu amor florecerá. ¡Comparte tus esperanzas y sueños para el futuro de tu jardín matrimonial!

# I Got You

I Got you, so trust I'll never hurt or forsake.

I Got you, as a lighthouse on the cloudiest of days.

I Got you, as a shoulder to cry on and as your rock.

I Got you, for a lifetime, like the hands of a clock.

I Got You.

# Te tengo

Te tengo, así que confía en que nunca te haré daño ni te abandonaré.

Te tengo, como faro en los días más nublados.

Te tengo, como un hombro para llorar y como tu roca.

Te tengo, para toda la vida, como las manecillas de un reloj.

Te tengo.

# I Got You

Share promises for your true love:

_____
_____
_____
_____
_____
_____
_____
_____
_____
_____
_____
_____
_____
_____
_____
_____
_____
_____
_____
_____
_____
_____

# Te tengo

Comparte las promesas para tu amor verdadero:

# You Are That Woman

You are that woman,
who opened this skeptics mind.
You are that woman, who made me ask,
"Where have you been all my life?"

You are that woman,
who forever intrigues.
You are that woman,
who brought this bachelor
down on one knee.

You are that woman,
with a heart of gold.
You are that woman,
who allowed me to love your soul.

You are that woman,
whose inner beauty can't be touched.
You are hope.
You are that woman.
You are that patient love.

# Eres esa mujer

Eres esa mujer
quien abrió la mente de este escéptico.
Tú eres esa mujer que me hizo preguntar:
"¿Dónde has estado toda mi vida?"

Eres esa mujer,
que siempre intriga.
Eres esa mujer,
que puso a este soltero
de rodillas.

Eres esa mujer,
con un corazón de oro.
Tú eres esa mujer
que me permitió amar tu alma.

Eres esa mujer
cuya belleza interior no puede ser tocada.
Eres esperanza.
Eres esa mujer.
Eres ese amor paciente.

# You Are That Woman

Share moments in your relationship that provided a foundation
of love and friendship:

_____

_____

_____

_____

_____

_____

_____

_____

_____

_____

_____

_____

_____

_____

_____

_____

_____

_____

_____

# Eres esa mujer

Comparte momentos en tu relación que proporcionaron una
fundación de amor y amistad:

_____

_____

_____

_____

_____

_____

_____

_____

_____

_____

_____

_____

_____

_____

_____

_____

_____

_____

_____

_____

# I See

I see your value.
I see your worth.
I see a little piece of heaven
that will now be my earth.

I see your heart.
I see your soul.
I see a love story,
that will never grow old.

I see a diamond.  I see a pearl.
I see a ruby.  I see my world.

I see a rose of timeless grace.
I see my forever, on this our wedding day.

## *Veo*

Veo tu valor.
Veo tu importancia.
Veo un pequeño pedazo de cielo
que ahora será mi tierra.

Veo tu corazón.
Veo tu alma.
Veo una historia de amor,
que nunca envejecerá.

Veo un diamante. Veo una perla.
Veo un rubí. Veo mi mundo.

Veo una rosa de gracia eterna.
Veo mi por siempre,
en este nuestro día de la boda.

# I See

Share how your true love nurtured and fed your soul:

_____
_____
_____
_____
_____
_____
_____
_____
_____
_____
_____
_____
_____
_____
_____
_____
_____
_____
_____
_____
_____
_____
_____

*Veo*

Comparte cómo tu amor verdadero nutrió y alimentó tu alma:

_____

_____

_____

_____

_____

_____

_____

_____

_____

_____

_____

_____

_____

_____

_____

_____

_____

_____

_____

_____

_____

_____

_____

*I* hope the love poems help you to find the perfect words for your true love, making your wedding day memorable, heart-warming, moving, uplifting, tender, sweet, sentimental, tear-jerking, warm, envied, touching and an example for other love struck eyes to personalize their vows. Feel free to use the poems during your first, second or third marriage ceremony, marriage renewal, Anniversary celebration or reconnecting moments to keep the passion alive.

"These poems are AMAZING and so hard to choose one as a Wedding Vow. Thank you so much for making my Wedding Day special.   You truly have a gift!!"                                        -Mrs. Jones-August 11, 2018 Charleston, SC

*Espero* que los poemas de amor te ayuden a encontrar las palabras perfectas para tu verdadero amor, haciendo que tu día de boda sea memorable, conmovedor, estimulante, tierno, dulce, sentimental, desgarrador, cálido, envidiado, conmovedor y un ejemplo para que otros amantes del amor puedan personalizar sus votos.  Siéntete libre de usar los poemas durante tu primer, segunda o tercera ceremonia de matrimonio, renovación de matrimonio, celebración de aniversario o momentos de reconexión para mantener viva la pasión.

"Estos poemas son INCREÍBLES y es tan difícil elegir uno para tu voto de bodas. Muchas gracias por hacer el día de mi boda tan especial. ¡De verdad tienes un don!!"                -Señora Jones-11 de agosto de 2018 Charleston, SC

# Author

Terri McCrea is a native of Charleston, South Carolina. She has provided counseling for the past 31 years (23 years of that in private practice). She graduated from St. Andrews Parish High School and the College of Charleston before receiving her Master's Degree in Clinical Counseling from The Citadel. She is an Adjunct Professor, a Licensed Addiction Counselor, a Licensed Professional Counselor, a Licensed Professional Counselor Supervisor, and servess as a Continuing Education provider for the South Carolina Board for Licensed Professional Counselors, Social Workers, Marital and Family Therapists, Psychologists, and Psycho-educational Specialists. She conducts local and national workshops on her 17 books as well as a Life Skills Summer Camp (ages five-18), parenting classes, domestic violence classes and anger management classes. She is the Outreach Coordinator of the Old Bethel United Methodist Church's Community Outreach Program that provides preventative, educational, rehabilitative, counseling, and evangelistic services to the Low country's at-risk youths, families, individuals, couples, elderly, poor, imprisoned, homeless, disabled, and indigent.

She writes mental health articles for local magazines, and newspapers. She guest appears for mental health segments on local radio and television networks. She can be described as a coach, counselor, visionary, poet, free spirit, and believer that everyone and everything has a purpose. She is a member of the Poetry Society of South Carolina (PSSC), the Old Bethel United Methodist Church Choir, Gamma Xi Omega Chapter of Alpha Kappa Alpha Sorority, Inc. and is a proud aunt and grand aunt.

She is available for book signings, charity events, public and motivational speaking engagements, workshop facilitation, interviews and expert appearances (radio, web, television and podcast) and poetry readings. She has self-published four self-help workbooks, four inspirational guides for couples in love, one parenting guide, four empowering guides for children, a mantra guide, a wedding vows book, a how to date book and her first collection of poems (2007-2020).

# *Autora*

Terri McCrea es nativa de Charleston, Carolina del Sur. Ella ha brindado asesoramiento durante los últimos 31 años (23 años de eso en práctica privada). Se graduó de St. Andrews Parish High School y del College of Charleston antes de obtener su maestría en asesoramiento clínico de The Citadel. Ella es una profesora adjunta, una supervisora con licencia de Consejería Profesional, y se desempeñó como proveedora de educación continua para la Junta de Carolina del Sur para consejeros profesionales con licencia, trabajadores sociales, terapeutas matrimoniales y familiares, psicólogos y especialistas psicoeducativos. Dirige talleres locales y nacionales sobre sus 17 libros, así como un campamento de verano de habilidades para la vida (de 5 a 18 años), clases para padres, clases de violencia doméstica y clases de manejo de la ira. Ella es la Coordinadora de Difusión del Programa de Difusión Comunitaria de la Iglesia Metodista Unida de Old Bethel que brinda servicios preventivos, educativos, de rehabilitación, asesoramiento y evangelización a los jóvenes en riesgo, familias, individuos, parejas, ancianos, pobres, presos, personas sin hogar, discapacitados e indigentes del Low country.

Escribe artículos de salud mental para revistas locales y periódicos. Aparece como invitada para los segmentos de salud mental en las redes locales de radio y televisión. Puede ser descrita como entrenadora, consejera, visionaria, poeta, espíritu libre y creyente de que todos y todo tiene un propósito. Es miembro de la Sociedad de Poesía de Carolina del Sur (PSSC), el Coro de la Iglesia Metodista Unida de Bethel, Gamma Xi Omega Chapter de Alpha Kappa Alpha Sorority, Inc. y es una orgullosa tía y tía abuela.

Está disponible para firmas de libros, eventos de caridad, charlas públicas y motivacionales, facilitación de talleres, entrevistas y presentaciones de expertos (radio, web, televisión y podcast) y lecturas de poesía. Ella ha publicado cuatro libros de autoayuda, cuatro guías inspiradoras para parejas enamoradas, un guía para padres, cuatro guías para niños, un libro de los mantras, un libro de votos de boda, un libro de citas amorosas, una guía matrimonial y su primera colección de poemas (2007-2020).

# Poetic Expressions by Terri

1643-B Savannah Hwy, Suite 113
Charleston, SC 29407
(main) 843.437.7572/(facsimile) 843.763.7202

*Visit:

www.btol.com, www.Amazon.com, www.Alibris.com ,
www.Abebooks.com or www.Booksurge.com

## Terri L. McCrea's Books

- The Power of Forgiveness: A Step by Step Guide on How to Let Go, Move on and Begin Living

- Problem Solving One on One: Proactive Tactics for Millennium Youths

- A Teacher's Dream: A Goal Setting Guide for Tots and Tweens

- The Joy of Living

- Unleashing the Lion: A Parent's, Teacher's and Counselor's Guide to Understanding the Verbal and Nonverbal Language of Children, Tweens and Teens

- I Wanna to Be...(Inspirational Quotes from Women in Love)

- I Wanna Be...(Inspirational Quotes from Men in Love)

- What Women Want to Hear {not just on} Valentine's Day but Everyday

- How to Stroke the Male Ego: (Words that Make him Feel like a King)

- It's Ok for Boys to...

- It's Ok for Girls to...

- Walk Like a King: 100 Virtues of a True Gentleman

- Elite Girls Wear Pearls: 100 Virtues of Strong, Empowered and Balanced Women

- Soul Encounters: The Collective Poetry of Terri L. McCrea, M.Ed., LPC  (2007-2020)

- Walking in Love: Wedding Vows for That Special Day

- The Book of Mantras: 100 Affirmations to Reframe your Thoughts and Retrain your Brain

- What Price Are you Willing to Pay for Love? 2003. 2004, 2nd Edition 2008 (Author house: ISBN: 1-418-6299-3 (e-book)/ISBN: 1-4184-3315-2 (Paperback)

# Expresiones poéticas por Terri

1643-B Savannah Hwy, Suite 113,
Charleston, SC 29407
(principal) 843.437.7572/(fax) 843.763.7202

* Visite:
www.btol.com, www.Amazon.com, www.Alibris.com ,
www.Abebooks.com or www.Booksurge.com

## Terri L. McCrea

- El poder del perdón: Una guía paso a paso sobre cómo dejar ir, seguir y comenzar a vivir

- Solución uno a uno para problemas: Tácticas proactivas para jóvenes del milenio

- El sueño de un maestro: una guía para establecer metas para los más pequeños y preadolescentes

- La alegría de vivir

- Desatando al león: Guía para padres, maestros y consejeros para entender el lenguaje verbal y no verbal de los niños preadolescentes y adolescentes

- Quiero ser ... (Citas inspiradoras de Mujeres enamoradas)

- Quiero ser ... (Citas inspiradoras de Hombres enamorados)

- Lo que las mujeres quieren escuchar (No solo) en el día de San Valentín sino todos los días

- Cómo acariciar el ego masculino: Palabras que hacen a tu hombre sentirse como un rey

- Está bien que los niños ...

- Está bien que las niñas ...

- Camina como un rey: 100 virtudes de un verdadero caballero

- Las chicas de élite usan perlas: 100 virtudes de mujeres fuertes, empoderadas y equilibradas

- Encuentros del alma: La poesía colectiva de Terri L. McCrea, M.Ed., LPC  (2007-2020)

- Caminando en el amor: votos matrimoniales para ese día especial

- El libro de los Mantras: 100 afirmaciones o Replantae tus pensamientos y vuelve a entrenar tu cerebro

- ¿Qué precio estás dispuesto a pagar por el amor? 2003. 2004, 2ª edición 2008, (Casa del autor: ISBN: 1-418-6299-3 (libro electrónico) / ISBN: 1-4184-3315-2 (Libro en rústica)

www.ingramcontent.com/pod-product-compliance
Lightning Source LLC
Chambersburg PA
CBHW021148090426
42740CB00008B/997